ANNE GEDDES™

ISBN 0-8362-8178-0

Published in 1998 by Photogenique Publishers (a division of Hodder Moa Beckett)
Studio 3.16, Axis Building, 1 Cleveland Road, Parnell
Auckland, New Zealand

First Canadian edition published in 1998 by Andrews McMeel Publishing
4520 Main Street, Kansas City, MO 64111-7701, USA

Designed by Frances Young
Produced by Kel Geddes
Color separations by MH Group

Printed through Midas Printing Limited, Hong Kong

ANNE GEDDES

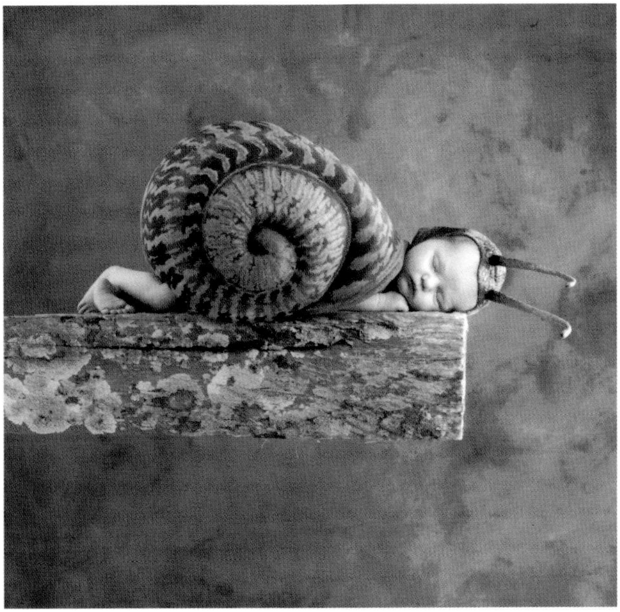

Journal

Andrews McMeel Publishing
Kansas City

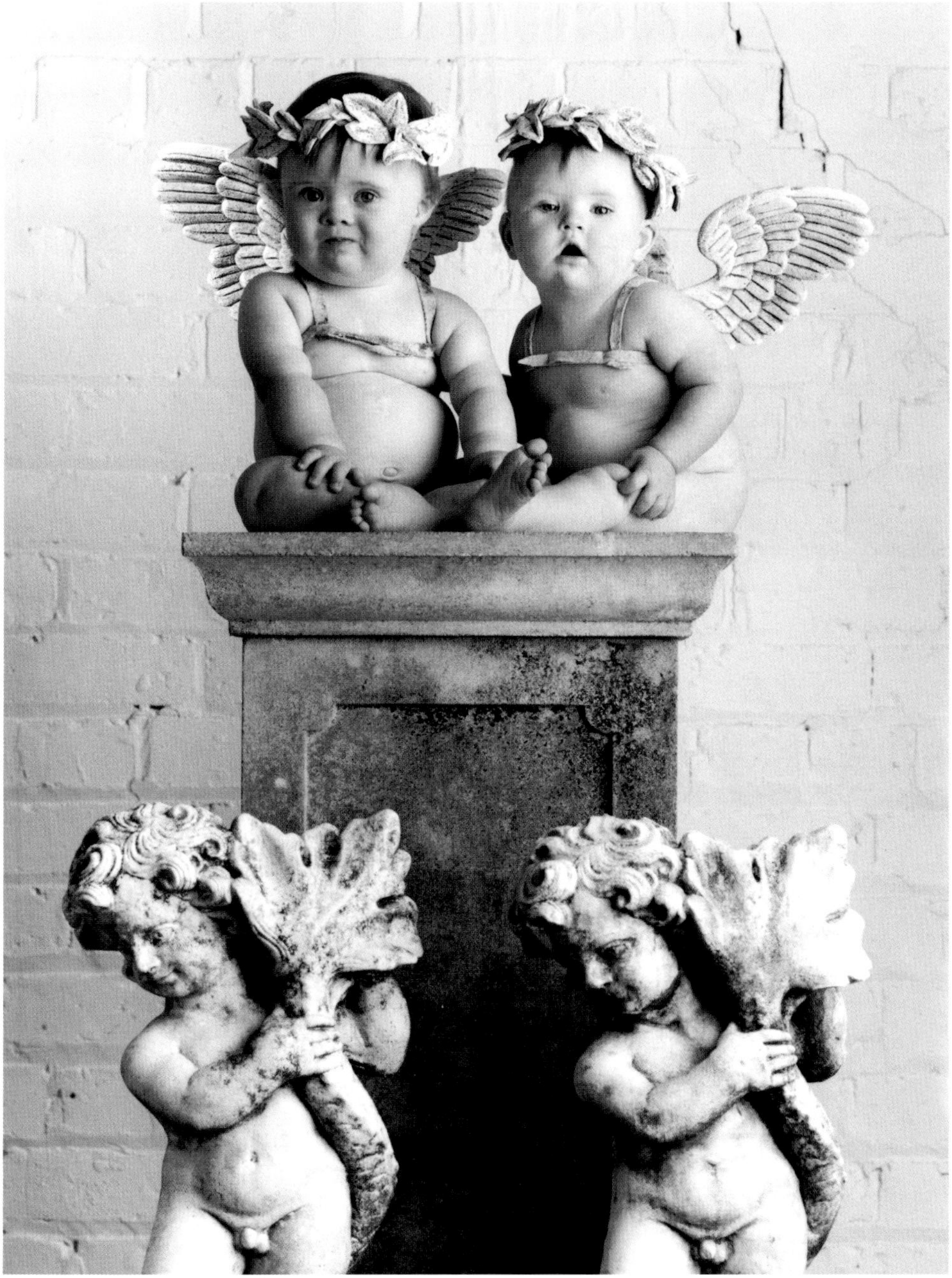

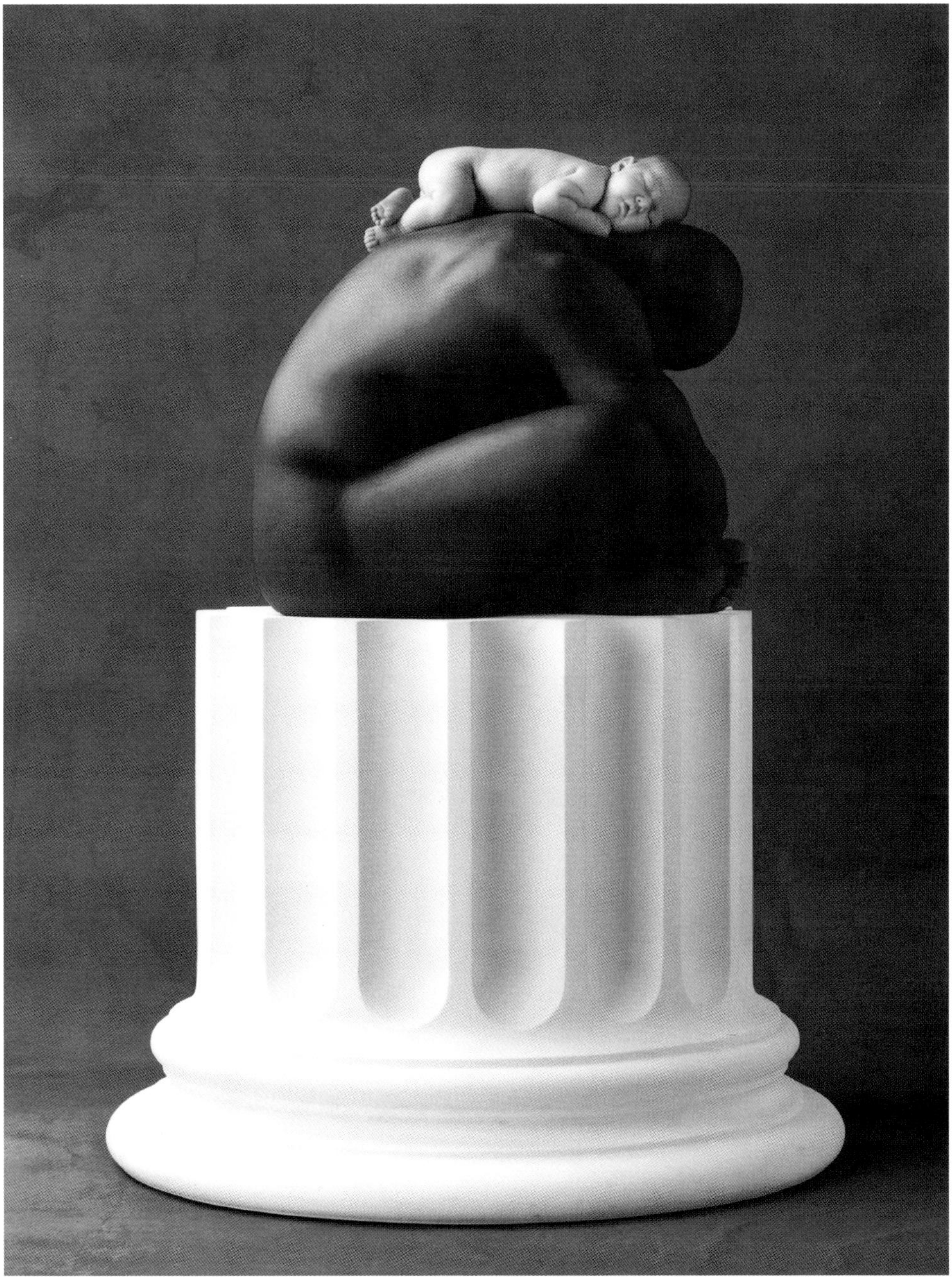

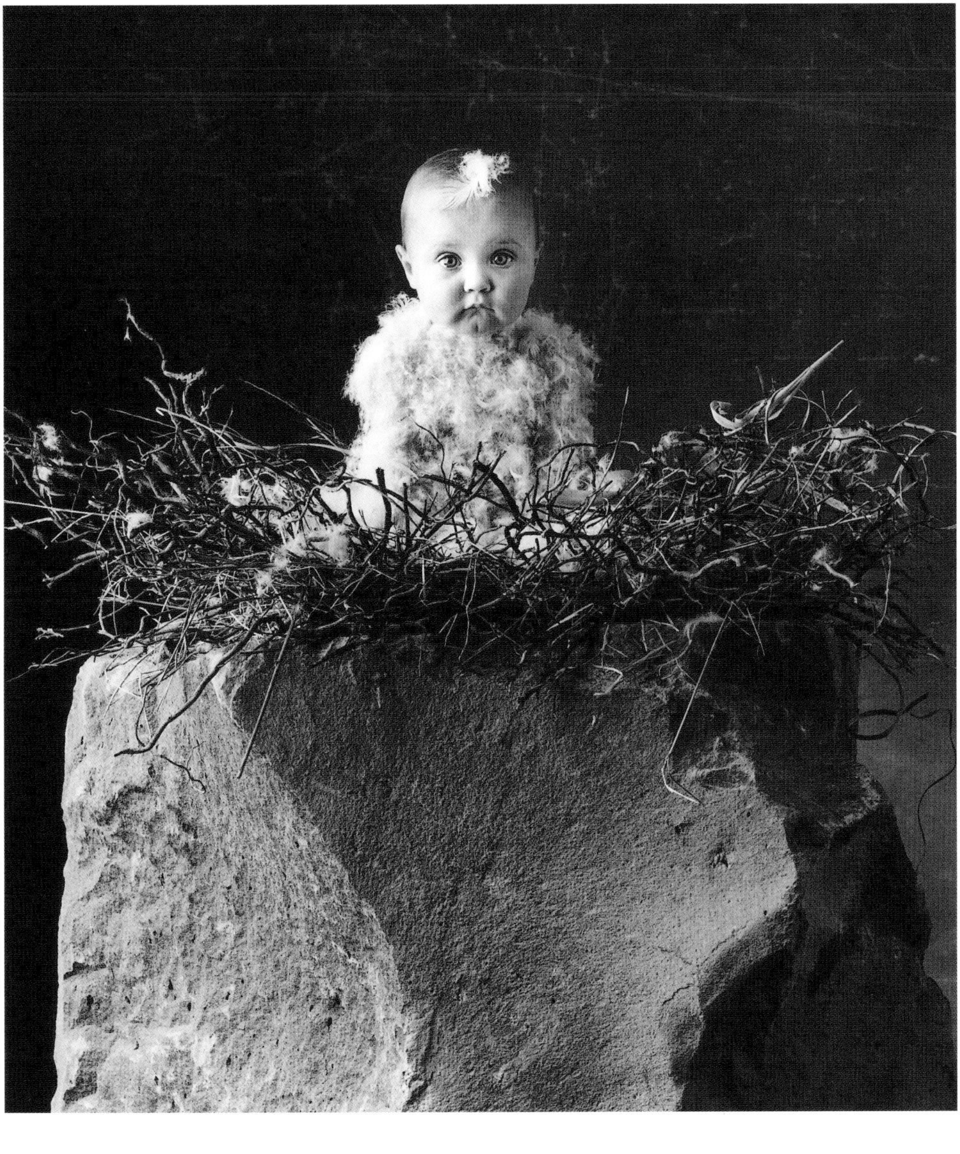

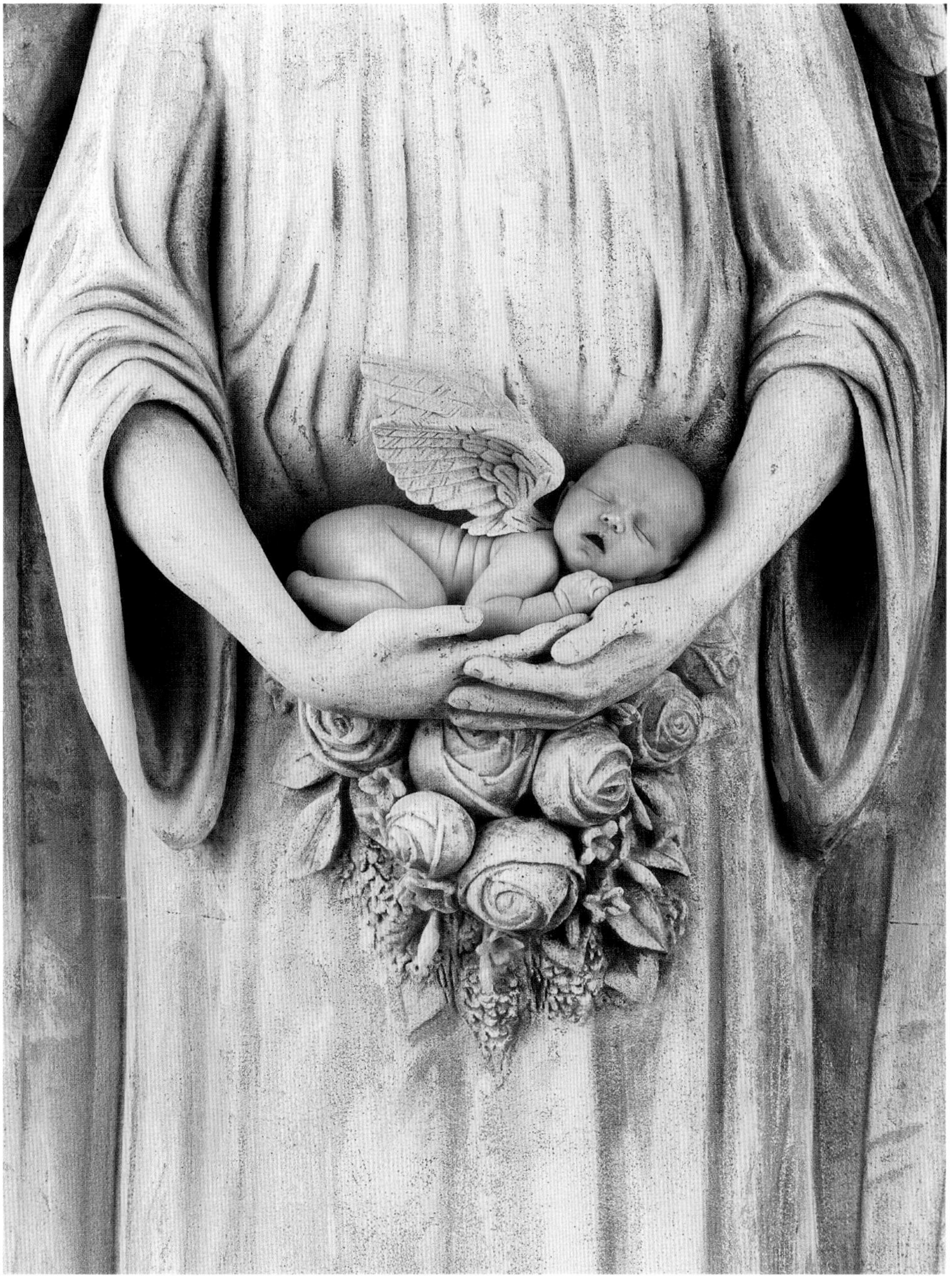

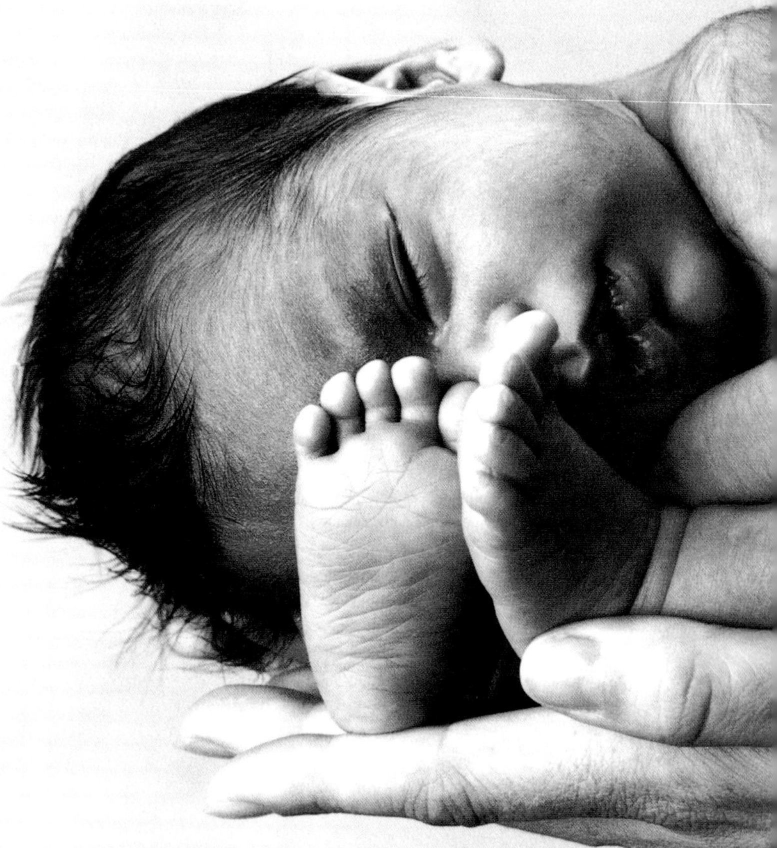

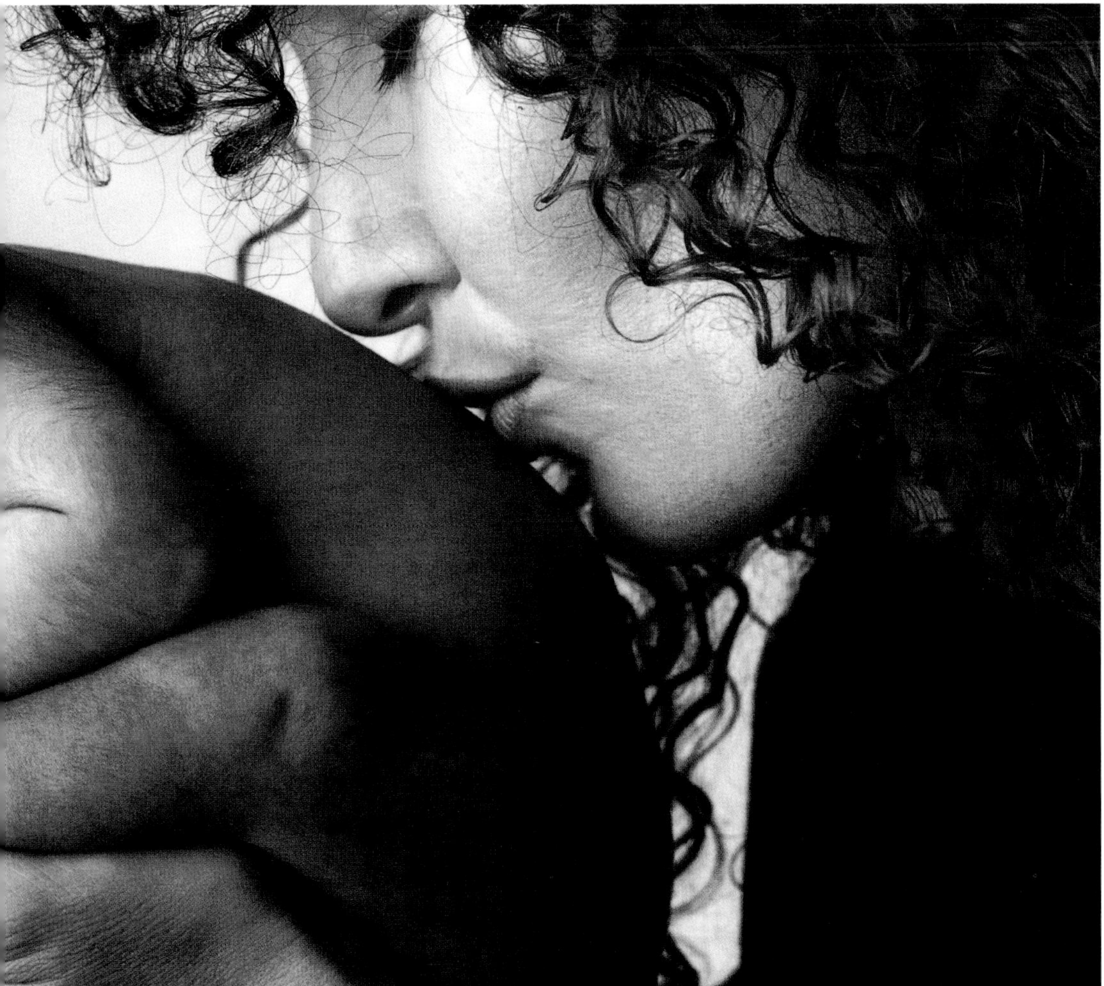

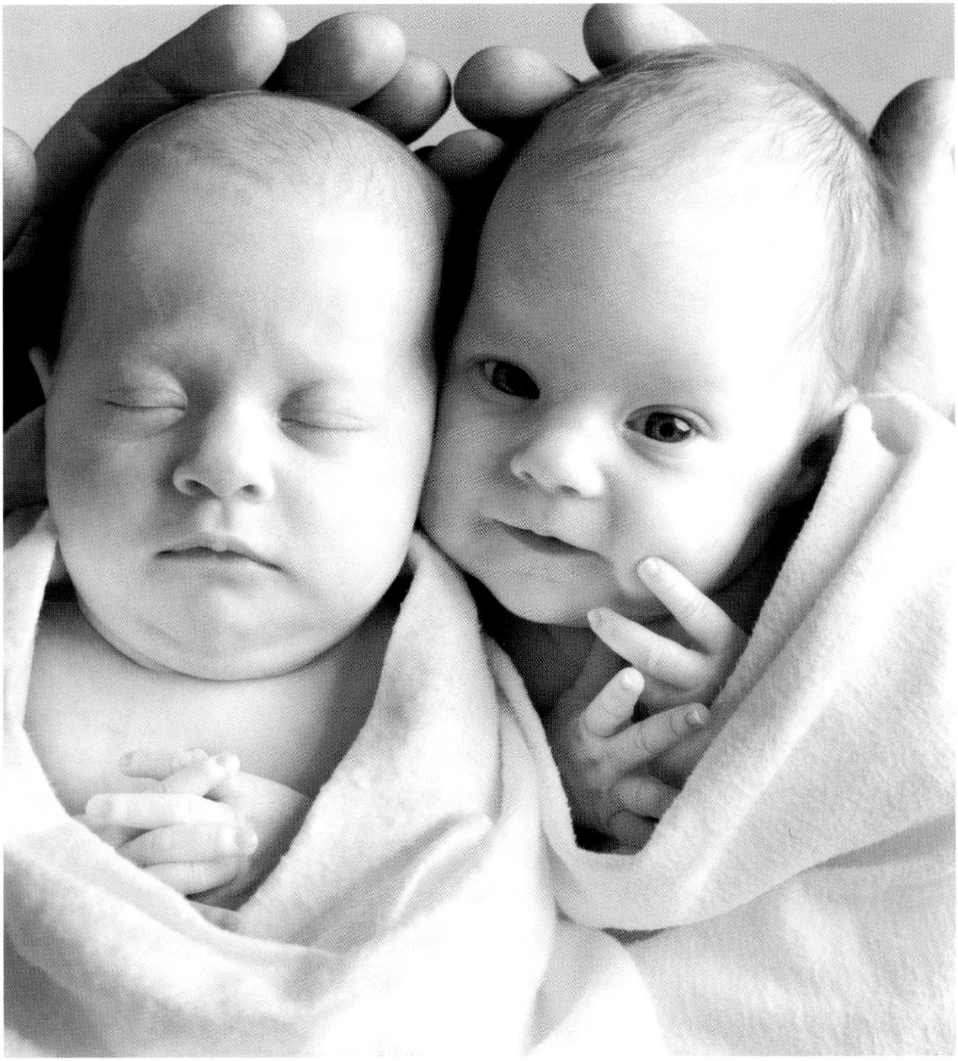

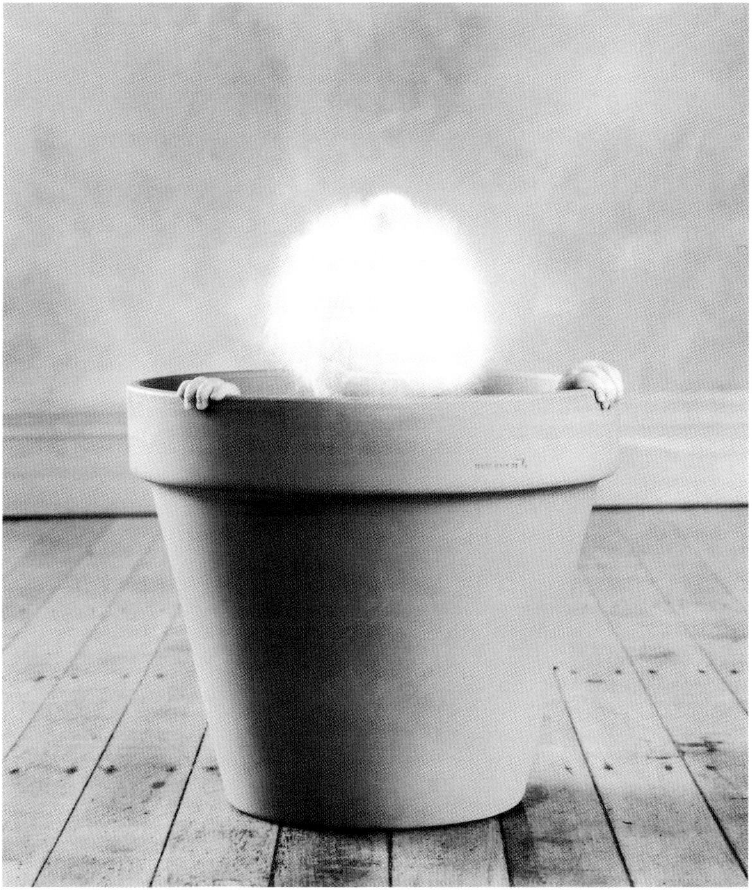

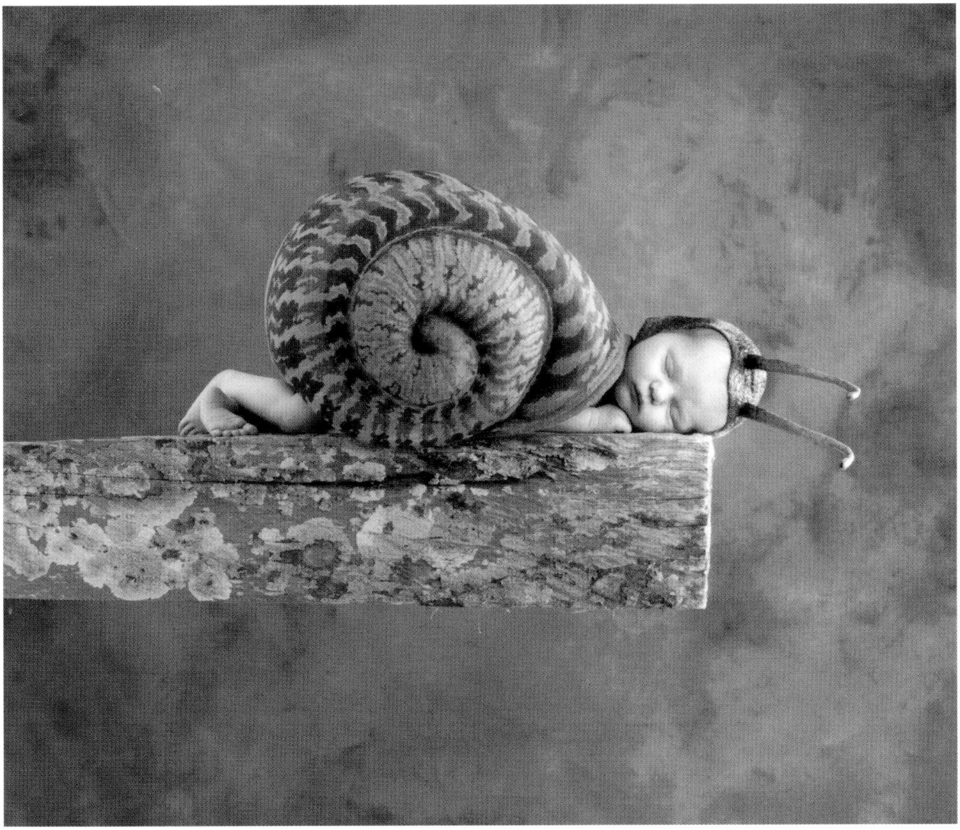

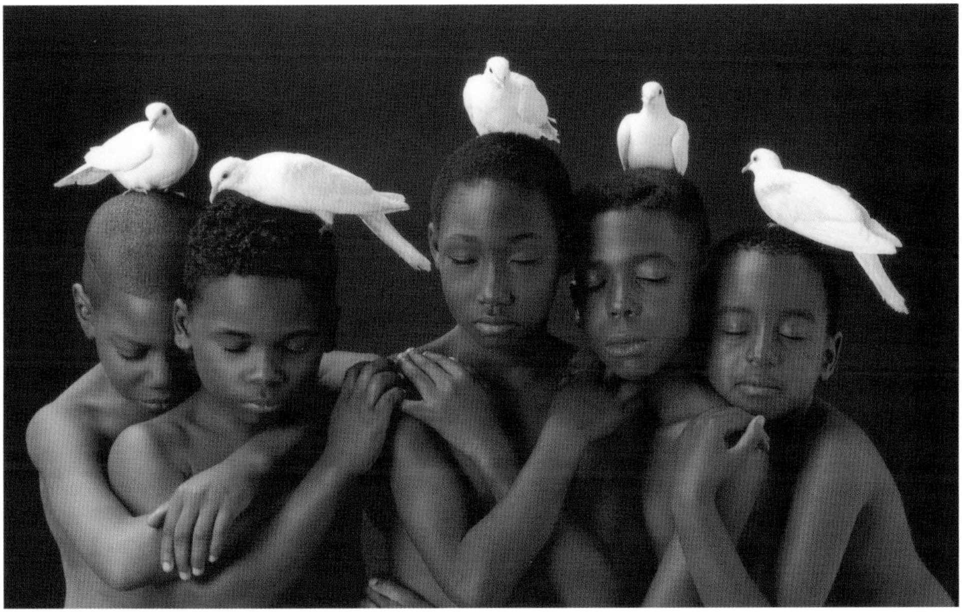

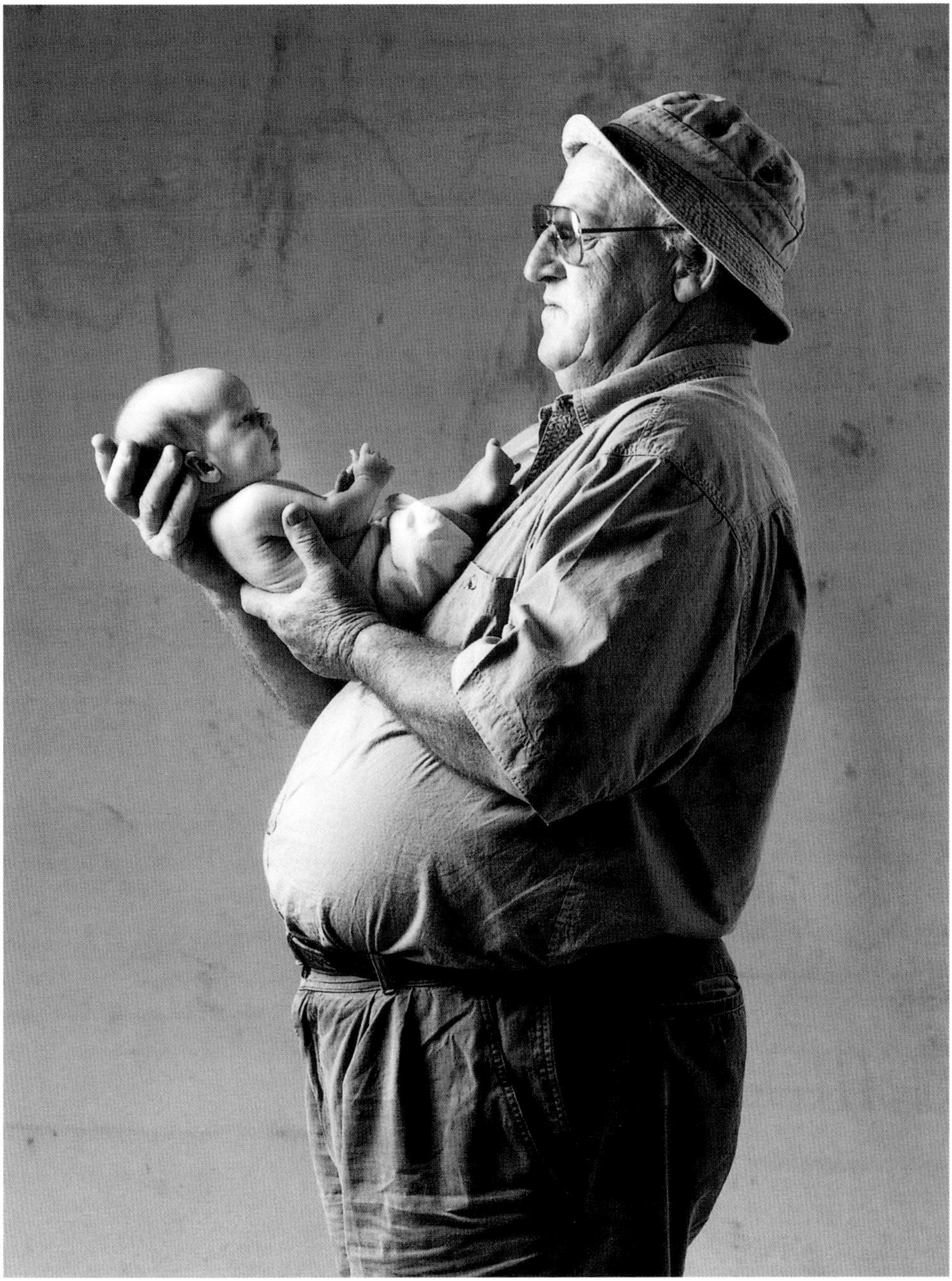

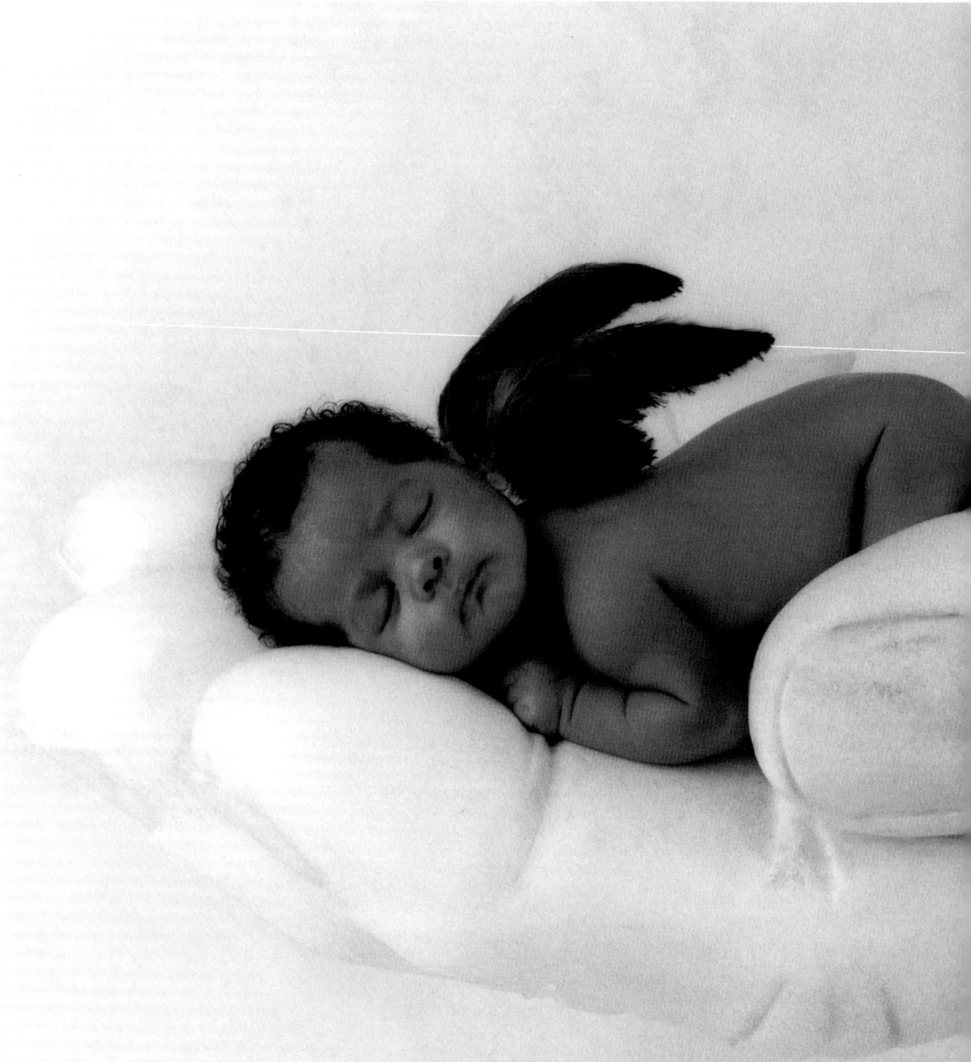

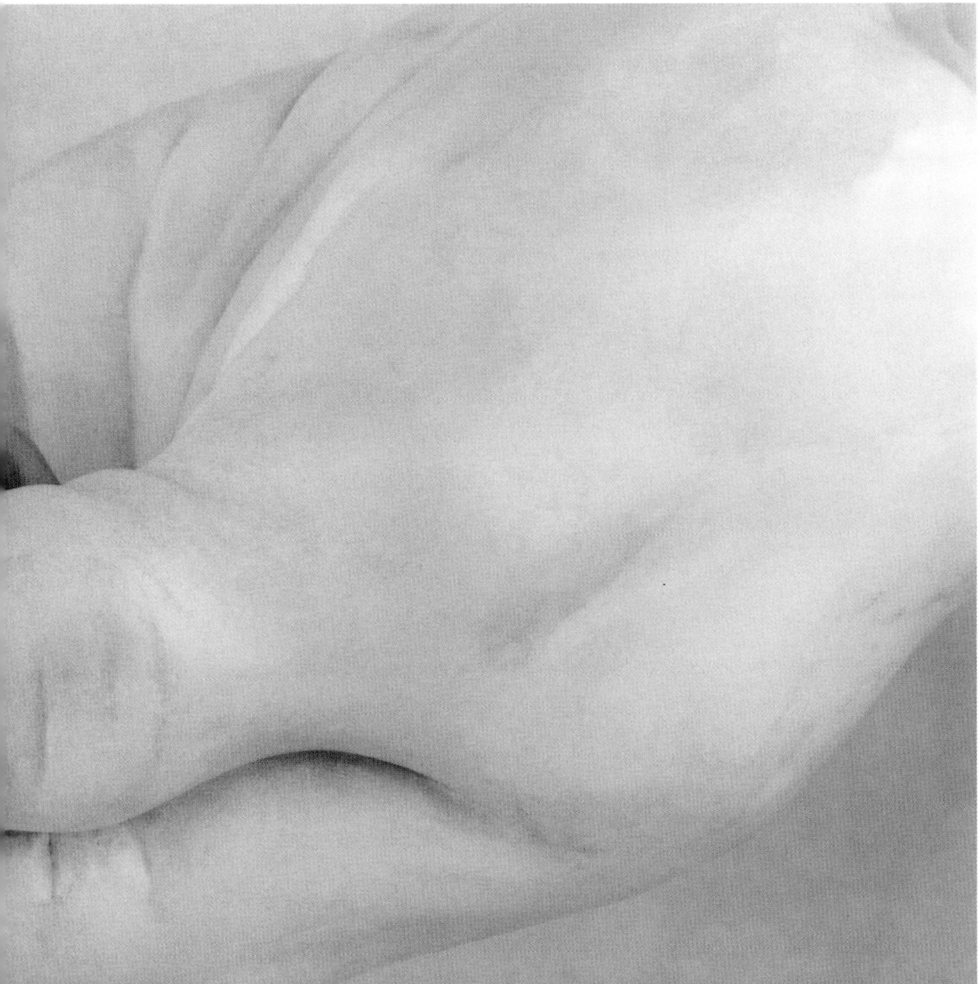

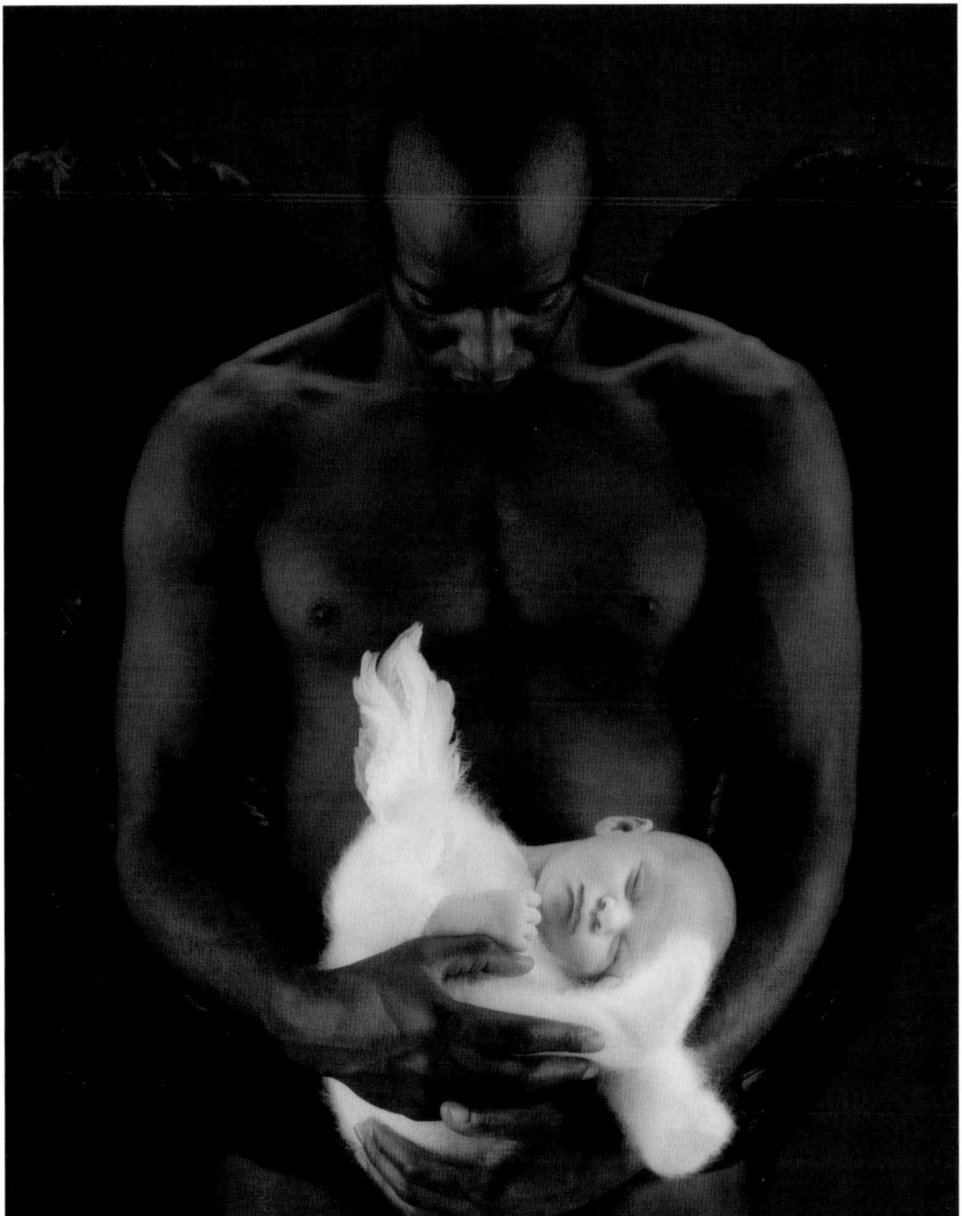

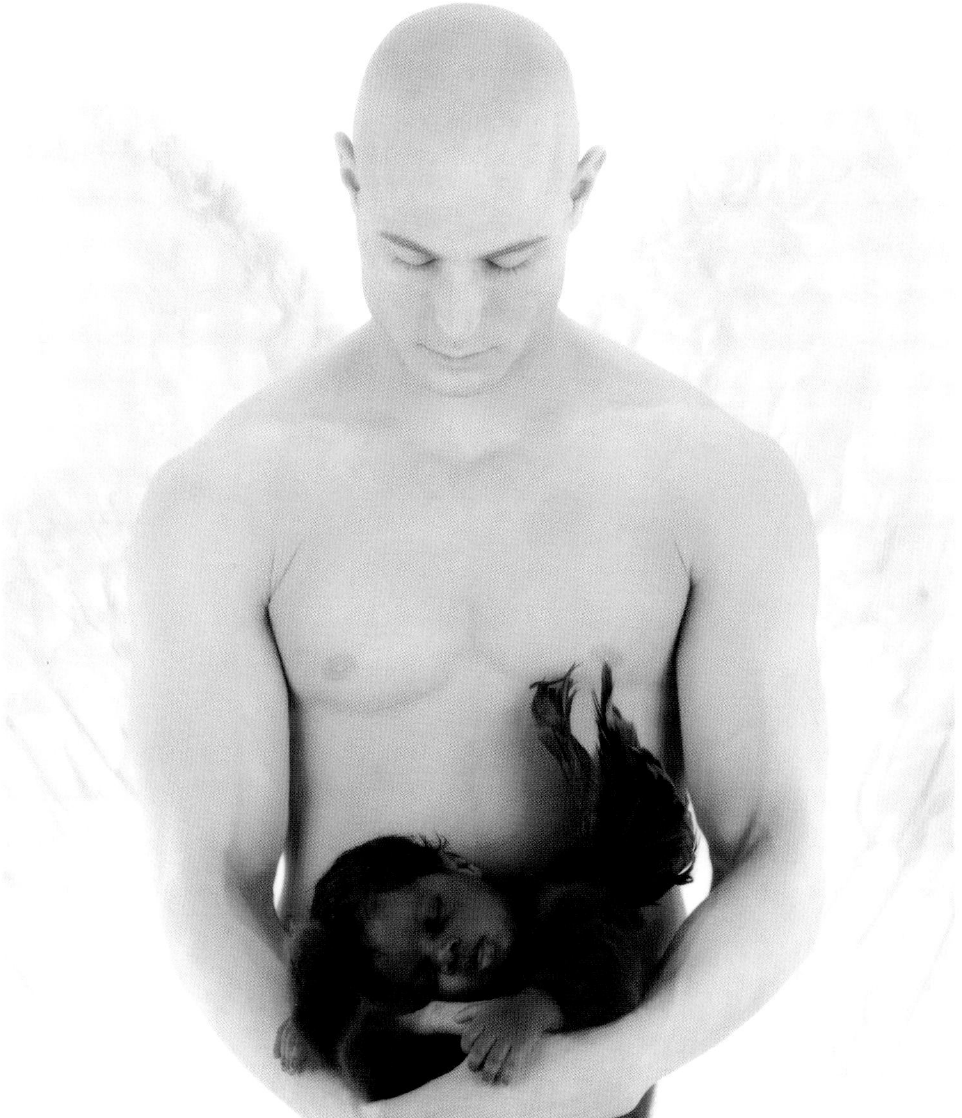

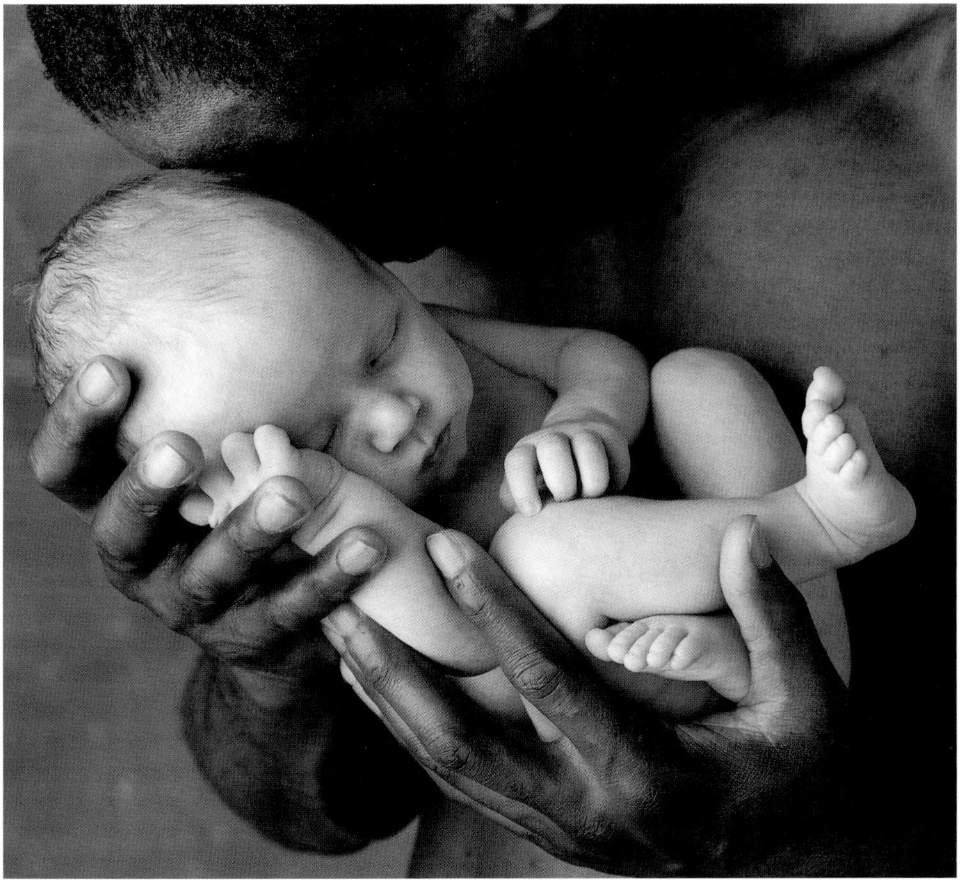

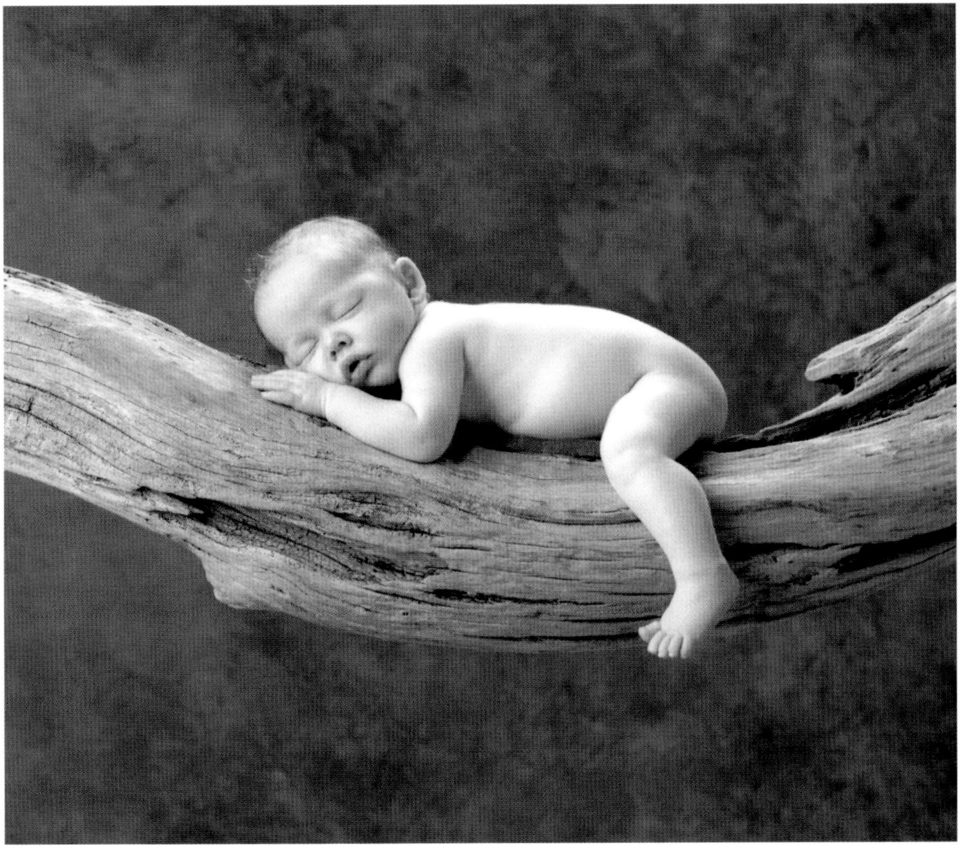

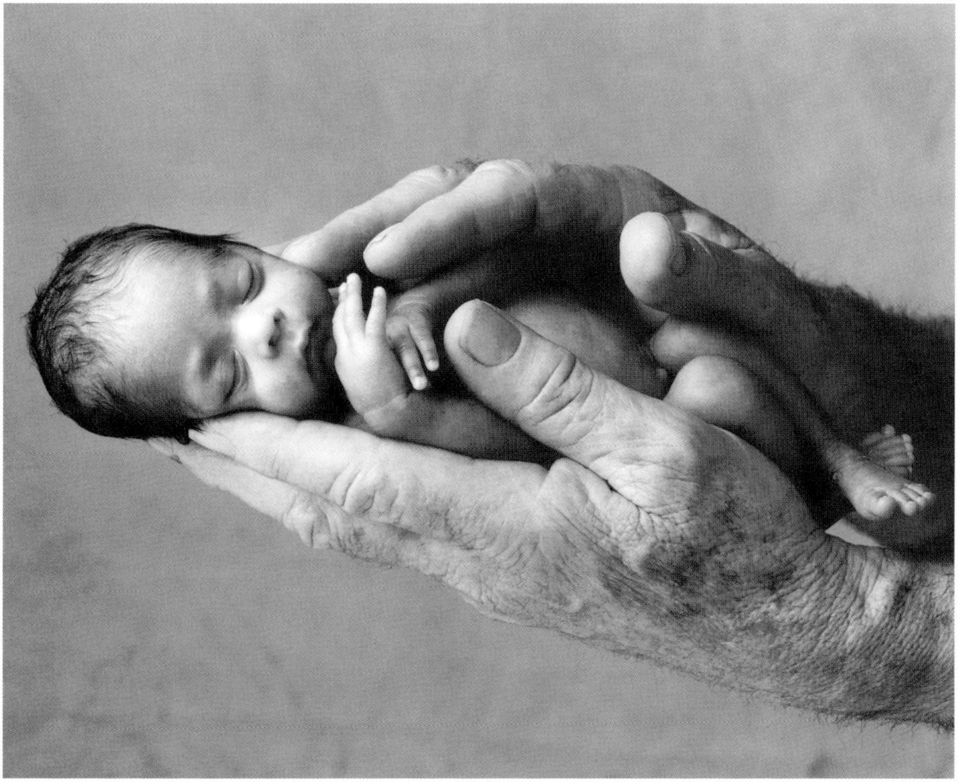

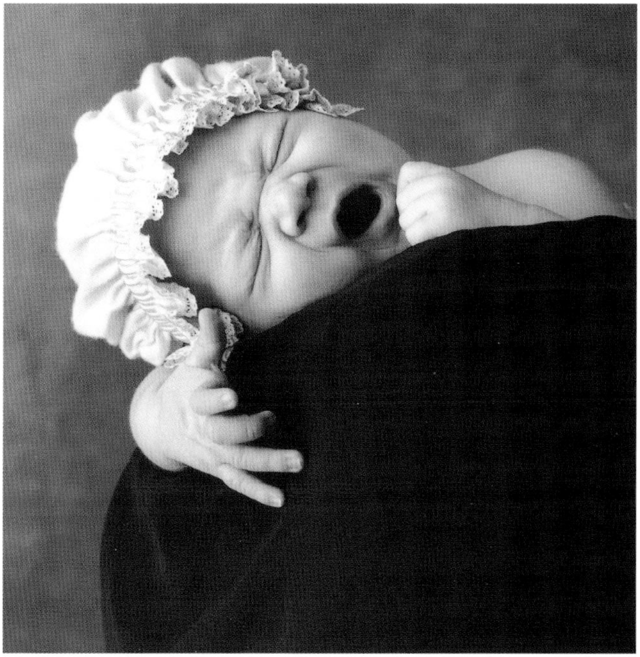

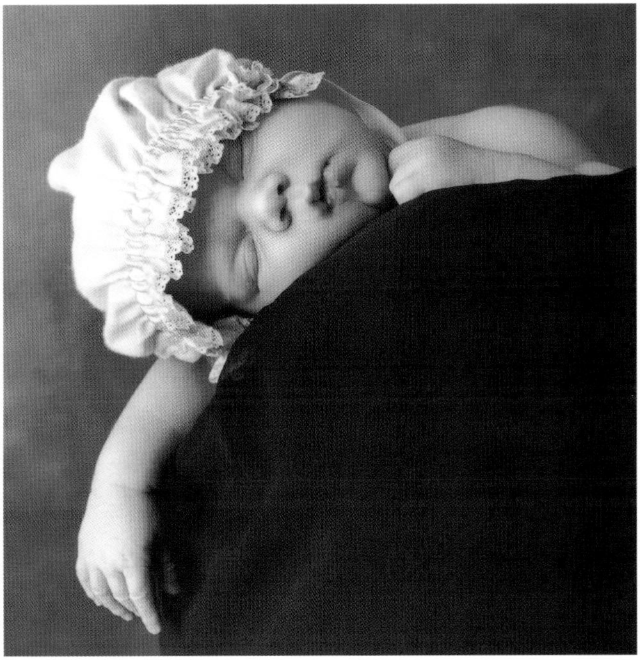

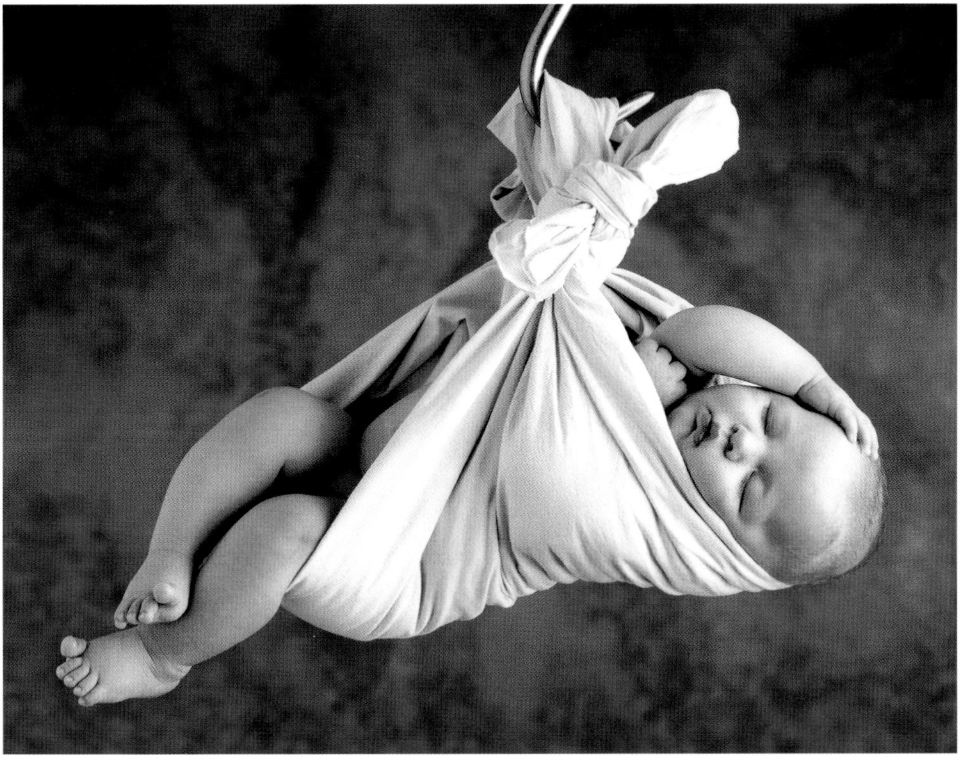

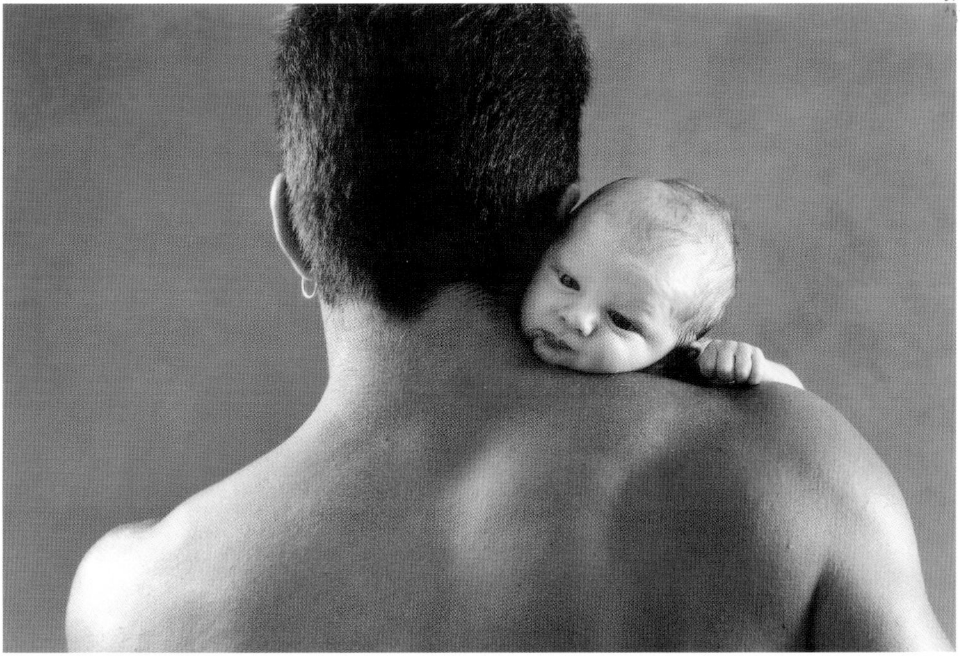

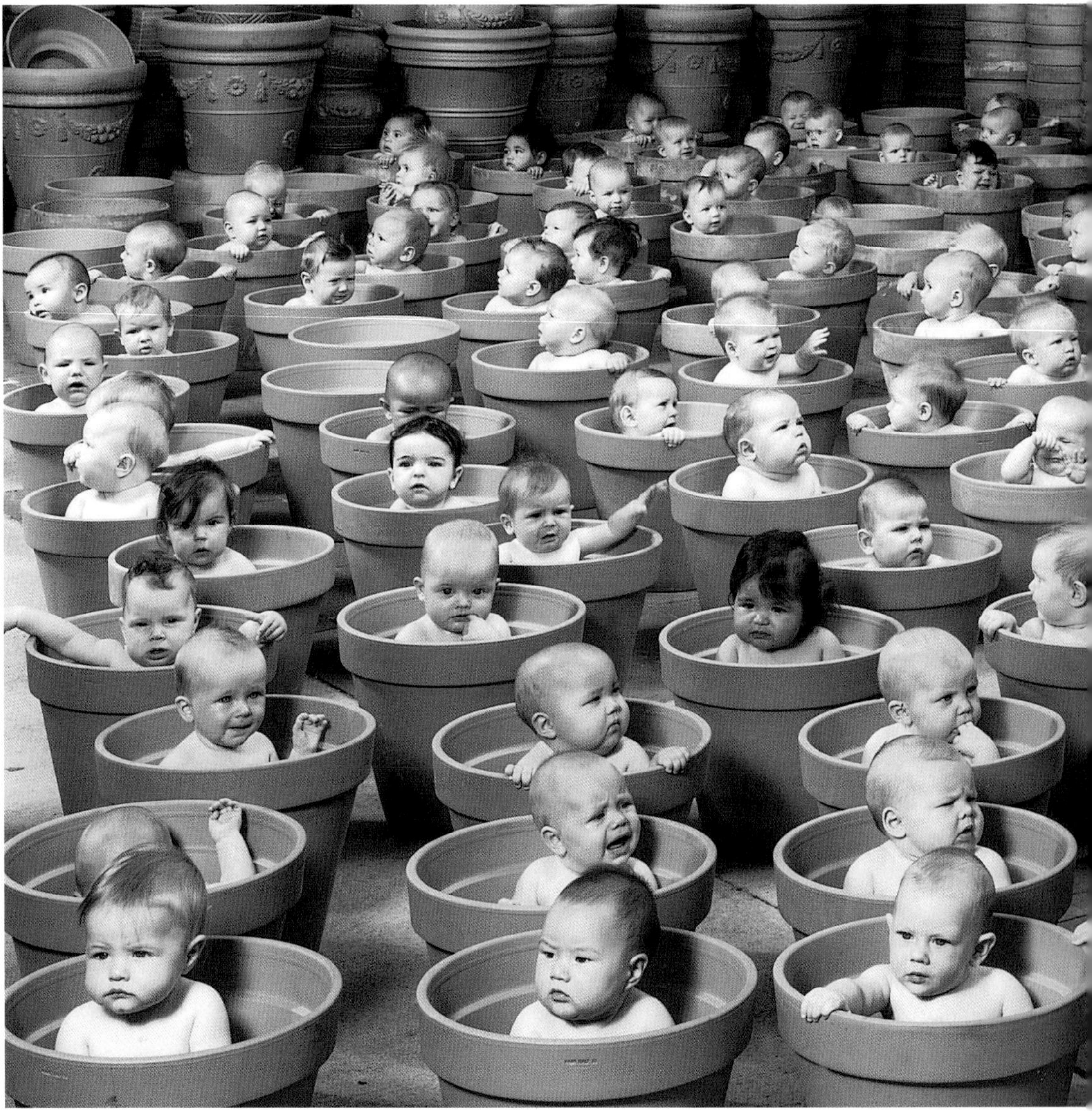

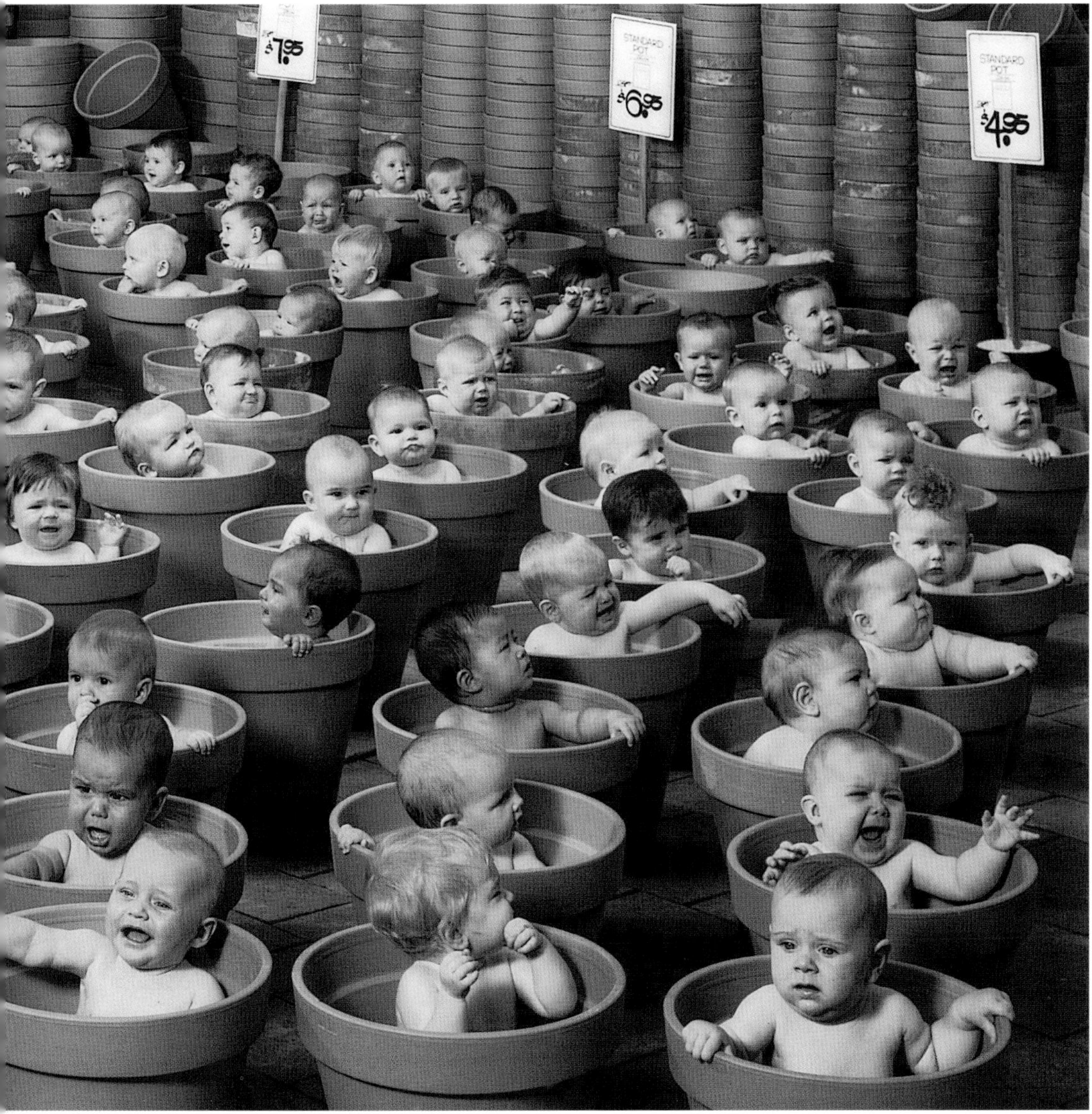
$7.95
STANDARD POT
$6.95
STANDARD POT
$4.95

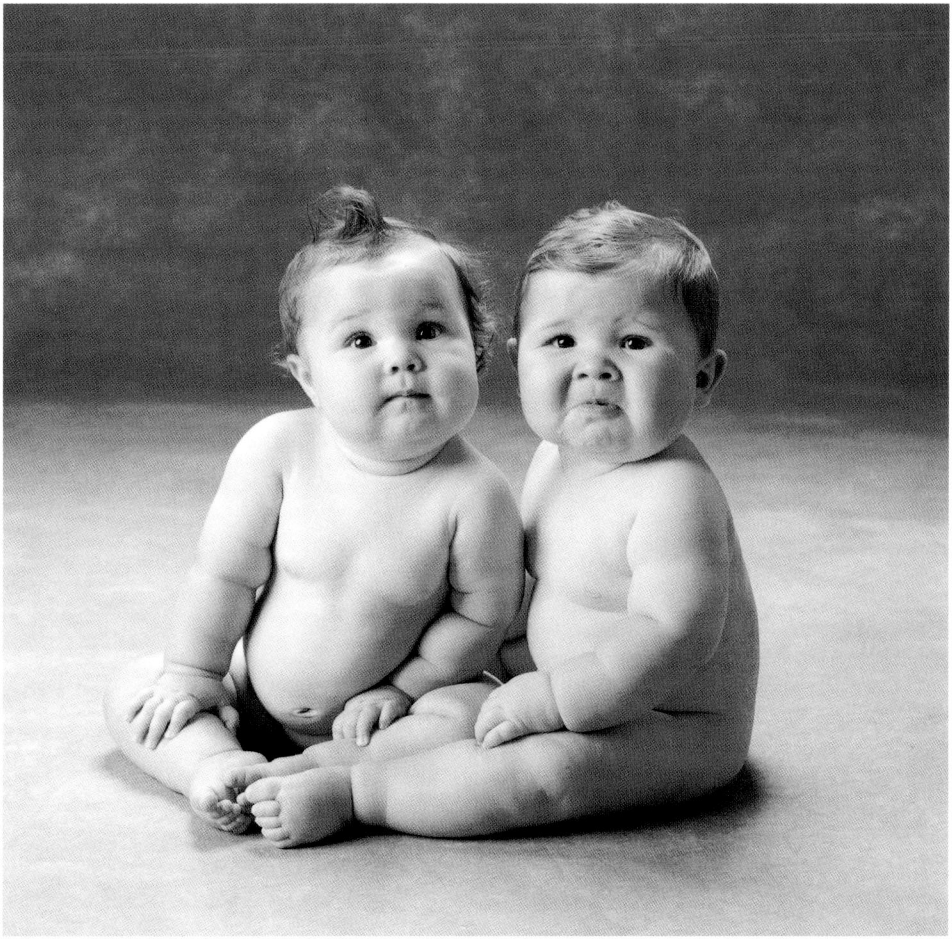

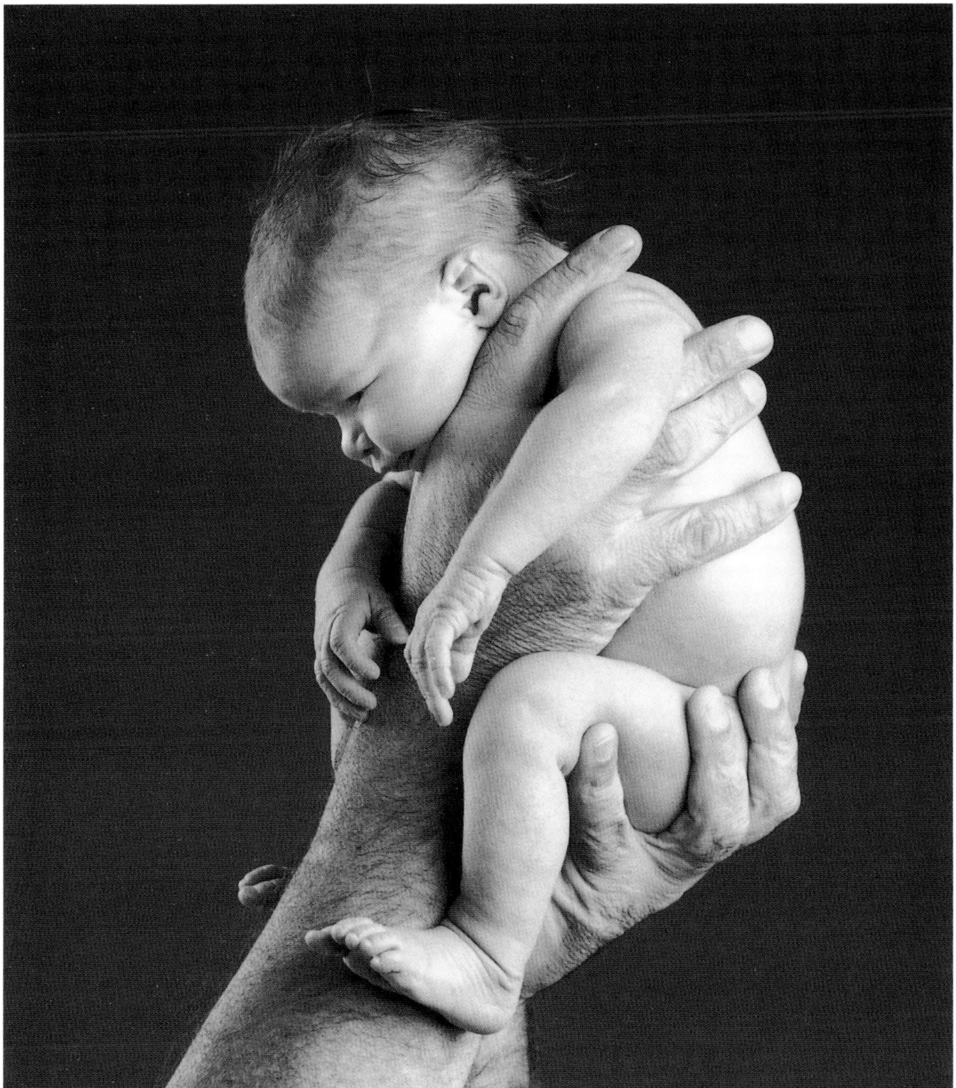

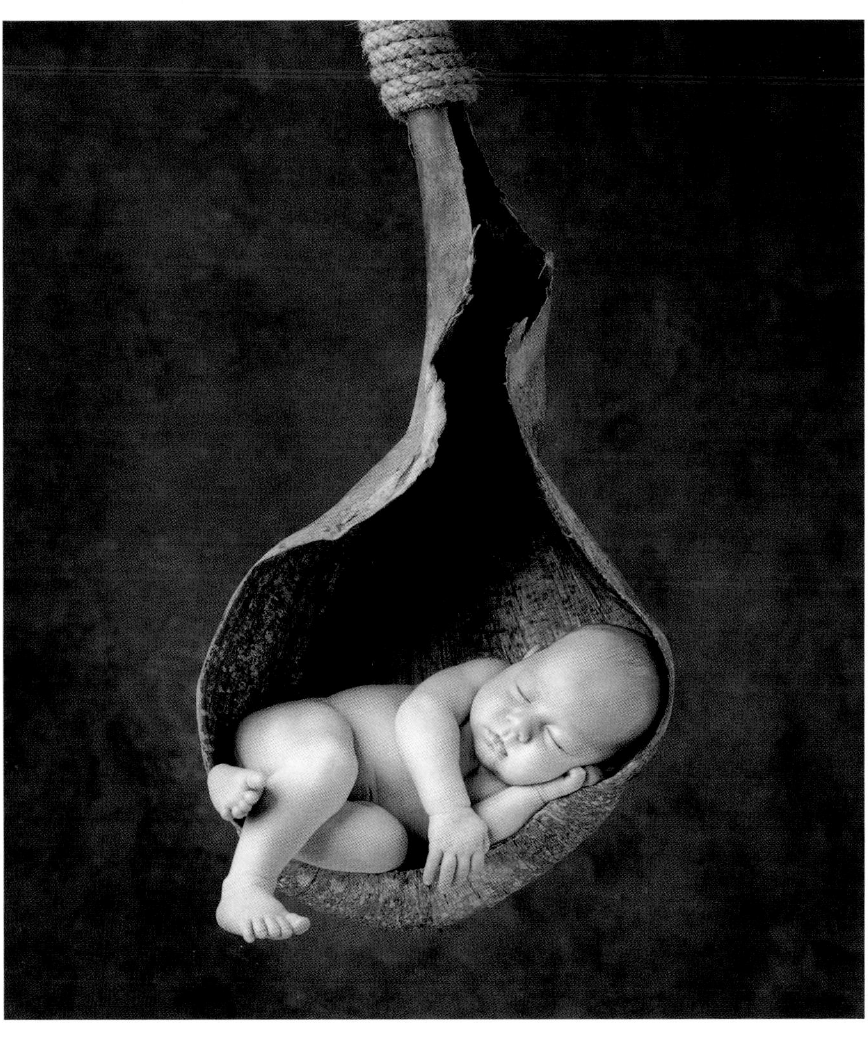